Published by Creative Paperbacks
P.O. Box 227, Mankato, Minnesota 56002
Creative Paperbacks is an imprint of
The Creative Company
www.thecreativecompany.us

Design and production by The Design Lab
Art direction by Rita Marshall
Printed by Corporate Graphics in the
United States of America

Photographs by Alamy (Gerry Pearce), Dreamstime
(Kitch), Getty Images (Tom Brakefield, Tim Graham),
iStockphoto (Michelle Allen, Carolina Garcia
Aranda, Tamara Bauer, Susan Flashman, Megan
Forbes, Joanne Harris and Daniel Bubnich, Pete
Karas, Christian Musat, Smileus)

The Library of Congress has cataloged the hardcover
edition as follows:
Riggs, Kate.
Kangaroos / by Kate Riggs.
p. cm. — (Amazing animals)
Summary: A basic exploration of the appearance,
behavior, and habitat of kangaroos, Australia's icon-
ic marsupials. Also included is a story from folklore
explaining why kangaroos jump instead of run.
Includes bibliographical references and index.
ISBN 978-1-60818-108-7 (hardcover)
ISBN 978-0-89812-693-8 (pbk)
1. Kangaroos—Juvenile literature. I. Title.
QL737.M35R54 2012
599.2'22—dc22   2010049210

CPSIA: 030111 PO1446

First Edition
9 8 7 6 5 4 3 2 1

AMAZING ANIMALS

KANGAROOS

BY KATE RIGGS

CREATIVE
PAPER BACKS

A kangaroo is a marsupial (*mar-SOO-pee-ul*). Marsupials are animals that are born in a pouch on the mother's body. There are six kinds of kangaroo. Two kinds are named "wallaroos," but they are kangaroos, too. All kangaroos live in Australia.

Kangaroos are some of the largest marsupials on Earth

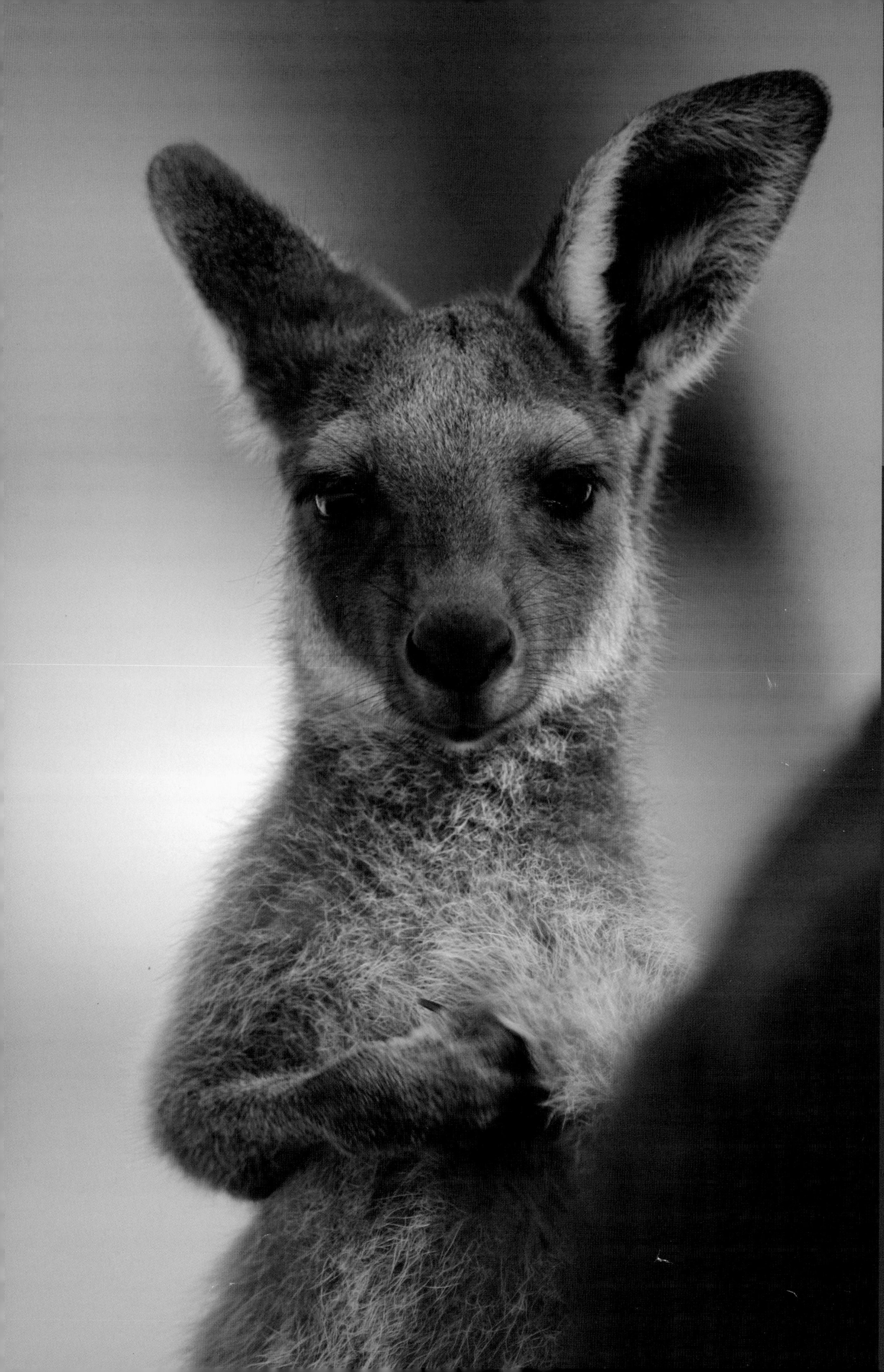

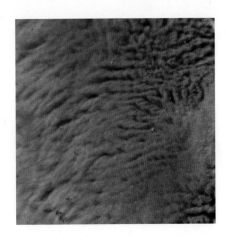

Kangaroos have big feet. Their bodies are covered in thick fur. Some kangaroos have gray fur. Others have reddish-brown fur. All kangaroos have long tails.

Red kangaroos are named for their reddish-brown fur

A male kangaroo stands 6 feet (1.8 m) tall and can weigh up to 200 pounds (90 kg). Female kangaroos are a little shorter and weigh less. Kangaroos jump to move around. They can jump as fast as 44 miles (70 km) per hour!

A kangaroo's strong back legs help it jump quickly

Red kangaroos live in the middle of Australia. It is hot and dry there. Grey and antilopine (*an-TIL-oh-pine*) kangaroos live in cooler parts of Australia. Wallaroos live in northern Australia. The land is rocky there.

Wallaroos leave the rocky cliffs at night to find food

Kangaroos eat plants like grass, **shrubs**, and leaves. A kangaroo eats about 15 pounds (6.8 kg) of plants a day. It has a special stomach with four sections. This helps the kangaroo **digest** all the plants.

digest to break down food in the stomach

shrubs woody plants that are smaller than trees

Joeys drink milk for about
their first year of life

A mother kangaroo has one **joey** at a time. A joey drinks milk from its mother. It lives in its mother's pouch for six to eight months. Then it starts eating grass. A kangaroo can live as long as 18 years.

joey a baby kangaroo

Kangaroos live in groups called mobs. Some mobs have only two or three kangaroos. Other mobs have 100! One male leads the mob. Other kangaroos act as **sentries**. They look out for danger.

sentries guards or lookouts

Sometimes kangaroos fight. They punch at each other like boxers. Most of the time, kangaroos eat and travel around. They spend a lot of time cleaning bugs out of their fur.

Kangaroos use their front legs to push and back legs to box

People in Australia have lived near kangaroos for a long time. They used to kill many kangaroos for food. Now, people like visiting kangaroos in the wild. It is fun to see these big animals jump!

When people think of Australia, they think of kangaroos

A Kangaroo Story

Why do kangaroos jump? People in Australia called Aborigines (*ab-oh-RIJ-uh-neez*) told a story about this. They said kangaroos used to walk on four legs like dogs. But when the first hunter chased a kangaroo, the animal could not run fast enough. So the kangaroo stood up on its back legs and started jumping. It jumped so far and so fast that the hunter could not catch it. Kangaroos have jumped ever since.

Read More

Bédoyère, Camilla de la. *Joey to Kangaroo*. Mankato, Minn.: QEB Publishing, 2010.

Markle, Sandra. *Outside and Inside Kangaroos*. New York: Atheneum, 1999.

Web Sites

DLTK's Crafts for Kids: Kangaroo Craft
http://www.dltk-kids.com/animals/mhoppy.html
This site tells you how to make a kangaroo and joey.

Ettamogah Wildlife Sanctuary: Make a Jumping Kangaroo
http://www.ausinternet.com/ettamogah/jumpkanga.htm
This site has a page to print for making your own jumping kangaroo.

Index

Australia 4, 11, 20, 22
feet 7
food 12, 15, 19
fur 7
joeys 15
jumping 8, 20, 22

mobs 16
pouches 4, 15
sentries 16
size 8
tails 7
wallaroos 4, 11